What's Left Behind?

Becca Heddle

OXFORD
UNIVERSITY PRESS

OXFORD
UNIVERSITY PRESS

Great Clarendon Street, Oxford OX2 6DP

Oxford University Press is a department of the University of Oxford.
It furthers the University's objective of excellence in research, scholarship,
and education by publishing worldwide in

Oxford   New York

Auckland   Cape Town   Dar es Salaam   Hong Kong   Karachi
Kuala Lumpur   Madrid   Melbourne   Mexico City   Nairobi
New Delhi   Shanghai   Taipei   Toronto

With offices in

Argentina   Austria   Brazil   Chile   Czech Republic   France   Greece
Guatemala   Hungary   Italy   Japan   Poland   Portugal   Singapore
South Korea   Switzerland   Thailand   Turkey   Ukraine   Vietnam

Oxford is a registered trade mark of Oxford University Press
in the UK and in certain other countries

Text © Becca Heddle 2006

The moral rights of the author have been asserted

Database right Oxford University Press (maker)

First published 2006

British Library Cataloguing in Publication Data

Data available

ISBN 978-0-19-917938-1

7 9 10 8

Printed in China by Imago

Paper used in the production of this book is a natural,
recyclable product made from wood grown in sustainable forests.
The manufacturing process conforms to the environmental
regulations of the country of origin.

Acknowledgements

The publisher would like to thank the following for permission to reproduce
photographs: **p4** Ancient Art & Architecture/Ronald Sheridan, **p5**t Corbis/Reuters, tr Ancient Art &
Architecture/Ronald Sheridan, l Corbis/Jonathan Blair, b Corbis/Ross Ressmeyer, **p6** Corbis/Jonathan Blair, **p7**t
Corbis/RF, b Ancient Art & Architecture/Ronald Sheridan, **p8** Art Archives, **p9**c Corbis/Jan Butchofsky-Houser, t
Charles & Jossette Lenars, **p10** Corbis/Ross Ressmeyer, **p11**tr & c Art Archives, b DK Images, **p12**t Ancient Art &
Architecture/Ronald Sheridan, b Topfoto/Roger-Viollet, **p13**t Bridgeman Art Library/Egyptian Museum, Turin, Italy,
Alinari, b Corbis/Mimmo Jodice, **p14**t Corbis/Araldo de Luca, b Werner Forman Archive, **p15**t Still Pictures/James L
Amos, b Werner Forman Archive, **p16**t Egypt Picture Library, b Ancient Art & Architecture, **p17**t Corbis/RF, b Art
Archives, **p18** Werner Forman Archive, **p19**t Art Archive, b Bridgeman Art Library/Egyptian National Museum,
Cairo, Egypt, Boltin Picture Library, **p22**t Corbis/Hubert Stadler, b Corbis/Reuters, **p23** Heritage Museum, **p24**
Corbis/Paul A Souders, **p25**t OUP/Classet, l Science Photolibrary, **p26**t Alamy/Jeff Morgan, b Library of Congress,
Washington, USA, **p27**t Vindolanda Museum, b Heritage Museum, **p30** Corbis/Martin B Withers/FLPA

Cover photograph: Corbis/Jonathan Blair

Illustrations by: **p29** Leo Broadley, **p24** Roger Gorringe, **p19**, **p20**, **p21**, **p28**, **p30** Lynne Willey/John Martin & Artists

Design by Chrome-Dome Design

Every effort has been made to contact copyright holders of material reproduced in this book. If notified,
the publishers will be pleased to rectify any errors or omissions at the earliest opportunity

Contents

Asking about the past

How can we find out about the past? You can ask older people what life was like 50 years ago, and they can tell you about time before that, from what their parents and grandparents told them. But we want to know more! We want to know about people we can never hope to ask for information – people who lived so long ago, there is barely any trace of them. How can we find out about them, apart from reading books? And where does the information in the books come from?

The answer is that what these people have left behind can tell us lots about them. Even if they lived before writing was invented, they have left their history in buildings, in the things they have made – and sometimes even in their rubbish.

This book is all about ways we can find out about peoples who lived long ago, and who have completely disappeared. In this book you will learn to find clues about the past from buildings, monuments, paintings, **artefacts**, tombs and bodies.

Why did they paint on walls?

4

Built to last

Some buildings and monuments made by people long ago have been built so well they have lasted right through to our time. You can visit them as a tourist.

Stonehenge, in the south of England, is a circle of enormous stones. It was completed about 4000 years ago, by **prehistoric** people. It must have been very important to them because they brought some of the stones from mountains 385 kilometres away – and this was before the wheel had been invented. No one knows what Stonehenge was used for, but on the longest day of the year, the sunrise lines up with its entrance, so it is thought that the structure may have had something to do with sun worship.

The great pyramids in Egypt were built as tombs about 4500 years ago. They are the only one of the seven ancient **Wonders of the World** still to exist. The pyramids were originally covered in white limestone, but most of that has been taken away to make other buildings.

According to a Greek historian, it took 20 years for 100,000 people to build the largest pyramid.

The Colosseum has stood in the middle of Rome in Italy for nearly 2000 years. It is an **amphitheatre**, where about 50,000 people used to watch gladiators fighting each other or wild animals. It could even be partly flooded for mock naval battles. It has been damaged by earthquakes and lightning, and by vandalism: all the marble seats and decorations are long gone.

After many years of restoration, it was reopened for performances in 2000 – there have been operas, concerts and plays shown there.

Lost cities

Some buildings from civilisations which existed long ago have survived because they are out of the way. If buildings are in the middle of nowhere, it is harder for people to build on top of them or to take the stone for new buildings.

High in the mountains

Machu Picchu was an **Inca** city and fortress, high in the Andes mountains of southern Peru, in South America. It was probably built over 500 years ago. Once, its temple and **citadel** were surrounded by terraced gardens joined together by about 3000 steps, but it has been badly damaged by time and weather. Machu Picchu was never found by the Spanish invaders who took over much of South America in the 1500s – it was only discovered in 1911, by a North American explorer.

Deep in the jungle

Tikal, in Guatemala, in Central America was an important **trading post** and religious centre for the **Maya** people. It has great temples and pyramids, and a form of writing on many of the monuments gives the date they were built – very useful to **archaeologists**.

The city spread beyond the temples, housing around 10,000 people, although probably 50,000 came to visit from the surrounding area. The city was abandoned some time around AD 900 and vanished into the rainforest until it was rediscovered in 1848. Now some of the forest has been cleared so the temples can be visited.

Why were the cities abandoned?
Historians have tried to blame outbreaks of disease, invasions, or changing patterns of trade – but no one really knows.

Buried alive

The wealthy Roman towns of Pompeii and Herculaneum sat under Mount Vesuvius. None of the inhabitants knew that the volcano was active until it erupted on 24 August AD 79. They didn't have much time to escape – we know this because when Herculaneum was dug up nearly 700 years later, coins and food still lay on the tables.

Pompeii was covered in ash and rocks when the mountain exploded, and Herculaneum was smothered by a mud slide. These cities were thriving at the time of the eruption, so their buried remains can give us a really good idea of what Roman towns were like.

We can see the style of the houses, how wide the streets were, what the markets and main squares looked like, even the counters of some shops. Pompeii had theatres, temples and an amphitheatre where gladiators used to fight.

Houses in Herculaneum affected by the eruption still have many of their contents. One house had a room divided by a wooden partition, which you can still see today.

The public baths have mosaics of sea creatures on the floors.

The archaeologists **excavating** Pompeii found holes in the ashes, left by bodies decomposing. They filled them with plaster and made casts, so we can see what people were doing when they were buried alive.

The walls speak

Paintings from the past can tell us a lot about the civilisations which created them. People have always painted on anything they could, with whatever they could get hold of.

Cave paintings

These paintings in Lascaux (say *Lassco*), France are thousands of years old. They show the kinds of animals the prehistoric people hunted. No food remains have been found in the painted caves, and this tells us that the painters did not live in them. They kept these caves only for painting – they must have been very important places.

Some images, like this one, show animals that probably did not exist. They suggest that the paintings had some religious meaning.

Tomb paintings

The pictures on the walls of Egyptian tombs show us the sort of clothes people wore. They also tell us stories – it is from these pictures that we can tell what they believed happened after people died and how they made mummies.

This picture shows the god of the dead, Anubis, weighing a dead man's heart. If his heart is lighter than the 'feather of truth', the man will be let into the afterlife. If not, he will be eaten up by the monster.

Pictures in houses

Pictures in Greek and Roman homes often show their legends and gods and sometimes tell us about everyday life. This **fresco** in Pompeii shows a cupid making things out of gold, using tools from the time.

Useful things

You have probably seen archaeologists on television, piecing together bits of broken pots to see what shape they were – the exact shape of a pot can tell them what it was used for and give clues about how it was made and how old it is. But many other useful everyday artefacts can also be found.

A well-equipped tomb

One of the amazing things about Egyptian tombs like Tutankhamun's is that they contain everything someone might need in an afterlife. As well as the statues and **ritual** objects, the tomb contained six real beds, lots of pairs of sandals, chairs, lamps, jars of wine, bread, grain, meat and other foods, including **chickpeas**, honey, and dried and fresh fruit.

The first tools

Flint tools are among the earliest artefacts ever made, so they are among the oldest things we can find. They have different shapes, depending on what they were designed for. Scrapers have a blunt side (to hold them by) and a sharp side, and arrow heads, like this one, are very easy to recognise.

Old stories as clues

Sometimes, old stories lead archaeologists to things that have been lost for hundreds of years. There was a legend that, hundreds of years ago, boats had been sunk to close a sea channel in Denmark. Archaeologists following up the story dug up this Viking ship and four others in 1962.

Arty things

As well as the things that past peoples made because they needed them, we can also find things they made for decoration or for religious purposes. These things can show us the great skill of the people who made them. They can also tell us about their customs and beliefs.

The Ancient Egyptians wore lots of jewellery – Tutankhamun's tomb contained many rings, necklaces and **amulets**. His mummy was wearing this bracelet when it was found. In Tutankhamun's time, jewellery must have been just as important for men as it was for women.

The Greeks and Romans left behind many statues, which you can see in museums. Many of them are of figures from their myths and legends. This statue is of the sea god, Poseidon (the Romans called him Neptune). He usually has a trident, and sometimes there are fish in his beard.

The South American cultures left very **stylised** art. Pictures like this one combine so many elements it can be hard to see exactly what they show.

It's easy to see this is a picture of a person, but what is he holding? Can you work out where his head ends and his headdress begins?

South American statues are often massive, like this one of a king. His face and hands are easy enough to spot, but the rest of him is covered in complex patterns, perhaps representing his ceremonial clothes.

Tomb raiders

The way people are buried can tell us about their lives and beliefs, and exciting tombs have been found all over the world. Probably the most famous tombs are the ones of the Ancient Egyptian kings and queens. It has been rare to find a tomb which contains all the things originally put in it, though. Robbers who knew where the tombs were usually beat the archaeologists to it – often by hundreds of years.

The tomb of the boy king Tutankhamun, who died in 1327 BC, had been robbed twice. But both times the robbers must have been interrupted, as most of the tomb's contents were intact when Howard Carter excavated it in 1922. The mask above is the most famous find from his tomb.

Tutankhamun's mummy was inside four coffins: a stone one, with three others nested inside it. The innermost one was made of 110 kilograms of solid gold. Inside that was the king's mummified body, wearing the famous gold and blue mask.

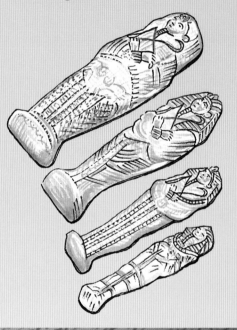

All around the tomb other things were piled up – practical items, like fans and equipment for writing and shaving, and model boats, dismantled chariots and thrones.

The most amazing thing was the number of statues – no other tomb had ever been found which contained so many. There were 35 of Tutankhamun and various gods, and 413 'shabtis' (servant figures) on hand to do any work that might be needed in the afterlife.

How to make a mummy

Although mummified bodies have been found in many different areas of the world, the most famous ones are those of Ancient Egypt. But how did they actually go about making a mummy? Here's a step-by-step guide to what you would do if you were burying an important Ancient Egyptian.

First, wash the body with wine and then with water from the river Nile. Then, cut a deep slash in the left side of the abdomen and pull out the organs – but leave the heart where it is. The dead person needs their heart in place for the next life. Put a hook up the nose and pull out the brain in pieces.

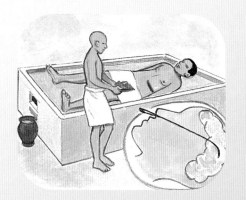

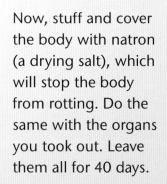

Now, stuff and cover the body with natron (a drying salt), which will stop the body from rotting. Do the same with the organs you took out. Leave them all for 40 days.

Wash everything with Nile water, and cover the body's skin with sweet-smelling oils to keep it soft.

Wrap the organs in linen and put them in **canopic jars**. Stuff the body with linen and other dry things, to give it a better shape. Then, wrap it up in linen strips and sheets, putting amulets in different places as you go. Now, it is ready for its coffins and tomb.

Canopic jars

The four jars are each for a particular organ.

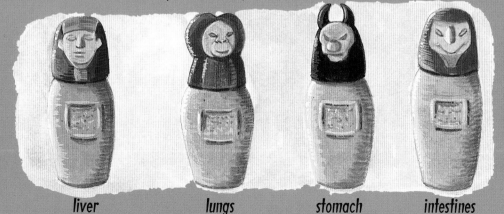

| liver | lungs | stomach | intestines |

Bodies

Mummies are the carefully preserved bodies of important people. But sometimes the bodies of ordinary people have been preserved by chance, and we can find out a lot from them – right down to what they last ate.

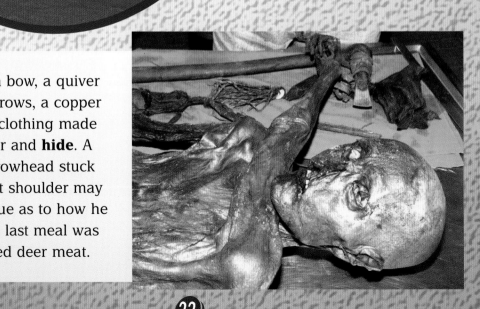

Two hikers found a body at the edge of a glacier in this Italian valley, in 1991. They called the police, thinking there had been an accident or a murder. But the ice man was actually over 5000 years old.

He had a bow, a quiver full of arrows, a copper axe and clothing made of leather and **hide**. A stone arrowhead stuck in his left shoulder may give a clue as to how he died. His last meal was mostly red deer meat.

Lindow Man was found in a peat bog in Cheshire in 1984. He died in about AD 200–300. The peat's natural chemicals had turned his skin into a sort of leather. He was naked apart from a fox fur armband and had clearly been murdered: his skull was smashed in two places, his neck was broken, and his throat had been cut. A leather thong was wound so tightly round his neck, he had probably been strangled too – perhaps all part of a ritual murder.

Naming bodies

Researchers like to name the bodies they work on. The ice man was called Otzi (say *Urt-zee*) after Otztal, where he was found. Similarly, Lindow Man was named after Lindow Moor – but, as a joke, researchers called him Pete Marsh.

Stories in bone

Some specialist archaeologists work on bones and examine them to find out about the people they used to be part of. These skills are even used as part of criminal investigations.

The size of the bones is an obvious place to start. Of course a child's bones are smaller than an adult's – and you can tell how tall someone was just from the length of their thigh bone.

An adult's skull or **pelvis** can reveal whether they were male or female. Women's pelvises tend to be much wider than men's, and men's skulls have ridges over the eyes. Which of these is the woman's pelvis?

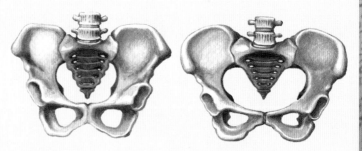

Teeth can give more clues about someone's age. Children's teeth grow and fall out at fairly predictable times, so a child's teeth can give their age to within about two years.

For adults, teeth can only give a very rough age. Young adults have no **wisdom teeth** yet. In older adults, how damaged the teeth are can be a clue – very old people's teeth may be missing or worn down by years of chewing.

The bones themselves change appearance in certain places when they stop growing, so we can tell if someone was still growing or not.

If bones have been broken, there are lumps where they have healed, like the area shown in red here. Or if they are still broken, that might be a clue as to why the person died.

25

Rubbish!

Did you know that rubbish tips can be really useful sources of information about the past? Archaeologists call them **middens**. Middens tell us about everyday life – the things that ordinary people made, ate and threw away.

In 2004, a Roman roadside rest stop was discovered in Germany, under a bus station. The middens gave good clues about the food served there. Most of the actual food had rotted away, but there were lots of bones and spice jars which still held traces of a popular sauce from Northern Africa. The bones showed that the visitors mostly ate chicken and pork, as well as bread, rice, **lentils** and fruit. The midden contained so many wine jars and broken plates it was clear the place was very popular and busy.

Another place where layers of rubbish have revealed fascinating finds is at the Roman fort of Vindolanda, near Hadrian's Wall close to the border of Scotland and England. Because the rubbish was sealed in with clay, things that would normally have rotted away have survived – from this child's sock to leather shoes, wooden combs and even the eggs of stable flies.

The most exciting find were the Vindolanda tablets: thin pieces of wood about the size of a postcard, with writing on them in ink. You'll find more about them on page 29.

I was there

Sometimes, people who saw events and cultures first-hand, long ago, have left us written accounts of what they saw. For example, the ancient Greek historian Herodotus (say *Her-odd-ot-us*) gave a description of how to make an Egyptian mummy.

When the Spanish arrived in Central and South America, they had to send back detailed reports to their bosses in Spain who were paying for the expeditions. So their letters home tell us quite a lot about the Incas, **Aztecs** and Maya.

We even have some accounts from the South Americans. Aztec spies wrote this report for their king, Moctezuma, describing a Spanish ship landing:

"We saw a house in the water, out of which came white men, with white hands and faces, and very long, bushy beards, and clothes of every colour: white, yellow and red, green, blue and purple; ...and on their heads they wore round hats."

The writers of the Vindolanda tablets were soldiers and their families. From what they wrote about, their letters could have been written yesterday.

The weather's bad so the roads will be terrible – I'm postponing that journey.

Come to my birthday party.

You owe me money.

I've sent you three pairs of socks, two pairs of sandals…

The kids send their love.

Visiting a site

You might get the chance to visit a really old place, in Britain or abroad. So how can you get the most out of it?

Some places are in ruins – many Roman remains only have the bottoms of walls. So you'll need to use your imagination (pictures of reconstructions may help) to build up a picture of life there.

Most importantly, soak up the atmosphere. Try to imagine what life was like there, and what the people were wearing and doing. And if you find one thing that you are really interested in, like a particular building or display, take your time to pick up all the clues it might give you about life in the past.

Glossary

amphitheatre – a round building with rows of seats rising around a central space

amulet – a small ornament or piece of jewellery, thought to provide protection against evil

archaeologist – someone who studies history by searching for and looking at the things left behind by people in the past

artefacts – things made by people in the past

Aztecs – a native people who ruled Mexico before the Spanish arrived in the 1500s

canopic jars – set of four jars used in Ancient Egypt to store the internal organs of mummified bodies

chickpea – a bean-like seed used especially in North African and Indian cooking

citadel – a fortress, especially one on high ground

excavate – to dig something out of the ground

flint – a hard grey stone that can be chipped or flaked to give sharp edges

fresco – a picture painted on a wall when the plaster was still wet

hide – dried or treated animal skin

Incas – a native people of the Andes mountains in South America, who controlled much of Peru and the surrounding countries before the Spanish arrived in the 1500s

lentil – a small, disc-shaped seed used in cooking

Maya – a native people of Central America whose civilisation reached its peak between about AD 300–900

midden – a historic rubbish tip

pelvis – the ring of bones that make up the hips

prehistoric – from the time before there is any written history

ritual – done for religious purposes

stylised – done in a way that does not try to make things look realistic

trading post – a place, often far from anywhere else, that people travel to in order to do business with each other

wisdom teeth – the molars right at the back of the human mouth, which do not usually appear before a person is 20 years old

Wonders of the World – a traditional list of seven amazing buildings and monuments in the ancient world. The list varies but was finalised in the Middle Ages: the pyramids at Giza in Egypt, the tomb of King Mausolus (the Mausoleum) in Turkey; the Pharos (lighthouse) at Alexandria in Egypt; the Hanging Gardens of Babylon in Iraq; the temple of Diana at Ephesus in Turkey; the Colossus of Rhodes (a huge statue standing over the entrance to the island's main harbour); the statue of Zeus at Olympia in Greece

Index